Time Management

Strategies For Efficiently Organizing Your Week And
Maintaining High Levels Of Productivity And Motivation:
Efficient Time Management Techniques For Enhanced
Motivation And Productivity

Royston Crawford

TABLE OF CONTENT

The Advantages Of Productivity 1
Cluttered Up Workspace 14
How To Find Greater Passion In Your Life 32
Boost Your Understanding 65
The Time Management Matrix Of Stephen Covey ..76
Examining Activities That Are Productive And Non-Productive 90
How To Beat Procrastination 118

The Advantages Of Productivity

Now that we know what productivity is, we will only be discussing personal productivity throughout this book and all of its chapters. This is your mission, your journey, your story.

Are you unsure of the benefits of productivity? The following are some advantages of becoming a very productive person:

1. There Is Increased Clarity

Things become much clearer when procedures are streamlined, methods are streamlined, and clutter is cleared out. It offers you an easier way to go about finding a solution. Why add to the already stressful nature of life by introducing disorderly routines, inconsistent schedules, labelless notebooks, and unhealthy habits? Take charge of what you can control. When you are productive, you are able to clearly identify the things that need to be completed, why they must be completed within a specific amount of time, and how they will be completed.

2. Your Concentration Will Be Improved

The majority of people on the planet struggle to maintain focus in the age of the internet. Without question, the internet, technology, and all the conveniences of 21st-century life are wonderful inventions that have saved many lives. When there was no internet, what did we do? How did we pass the time as we waited for a visitor? How did we obtain the news each day? With so much information at our fingertips, it's simple to find distractions and entice people to divert from their goals. All it takes for our attention to be diverted from the task at hand is a ping on your laptop or a ring on your cell phone.

A stressed and unproductive life is the result of not being able to focus on what is essential and what has to be done. The secret to productivity is focus. When you stay focused, you give your task the proper amount of time and perspective while also paying attention to the most crucial parts of it. Less time and effort will be required to produce more.

3. You're Stress-Free

You can manage stress and tiredness better when you are clear-headed and focused. All of us want a life free from stress, don't we? We already face a lot of stress from external factors like traffic congestion, everyday commutes, and never-ending work. Most people believe that hard work and success go hand in hand. Hard work is defined as working long hours and sacrificing other aspects of one's life, including family, friends, and physical and mental well-being when all you really need to do is work more efficiently and better manage your time. You can allocate your time and energy between vital and irrelevant tasks when you are productive. It's not necessary to give up everything in your life in order to do a single objective. You will be far more in control of what demands your immediate attention and what requires more work, and you will have a stronger grasp on life's priorities.

4. You Have Much Greater Efficiency

Many people wind up compromising quality for quantity when it comes to work. Many people have the tendency to neglect crucial components of a task in their quest to complete more chores, which can result in errors, mistakes, and subpar quality. Getting things done more effectively is one of productivity's perks in this regard. You'll be more adept at focusing and have a clearer understanding of what has to be accomplished for each work when you have clarity and focus. Better quality work is the result of this. You may produce more effectively and of higher quality when your attention and efforts are focused in one place.

When notes are spread over several notebooks, tags are very useful. It lessens the need to access comparable notes by opening multiple notebooks. To produce:

To tag a note, open it.

Next, launch the tag editor.

Choose the Click to Add Tags option for desktop applications on Mac or Windows. This can be found at the right part of the Evernote Notebook name, at the top of the opened note.

Click More... and choose Add Tag for iPhone, iPod Touch, and iPad. This is found beneath the title of the note.

On an Android device, search for "..." at the top of the memo. After clicking, choose Tags.

In the upper right corner of the note, for web browsers, click Info and choose "+" Tags.

Enter the desired tag text.

Click the Back button. Now, the tag will be added.

Press the backspace key over the tag to remove it.

Tags facilitate quick and simple note access, particularly when managing a large number of notes. For instance, many notes were taken during the course of a week, including a to-do list and a few notes on work. Different notebooks would be used, such as one for lists of purchases, one for to-do lists at home, and one for tasks at the workplace. Tag these notebooks for easy searches to access them all at once. Put a tag on these like "tag:\todo week1". All of the information stored in these several notebooks can be retrieved simultaneously by simply typing "todo week 1" into the search field.

To tag a note is to write a brief code on it so that it may be found more easily. It's similar to attaching a little label, such as a red flag, to a message to make it easier to find when needed.

All it does is categorize notes according to topics with this functionality. It facilitates the finding of all notes—texts, documents, photos, audio, etc.—that are connected to one another. Evernote will still search through every item in the note, but tagging will make it easier and more focused.

Evernote also boasts a robust search feature. It can even identify and look up words included within photos. For instance, if Evernote has stored copies of receipts in notebooks, you can search for a certain receipt by typing its text into the search field. Evernote will then find the precise text in all of the recorded receipt photos, saving you the trouble of looking through each one individually.

Gratitude

The web entrepreneur experiences a general sense of satisfaction and accomplishment when finishing a task. The sense of accomplishment serves as a catalyst, giving him or her the inspiration needed to either approach a new client or cultivate more business with existing ones.

These elements frequently serve as incentives for people working from home to manage their time effectively and come up with creative methods to solve problems more quickly. Often, an entrepreneur can better analyze his business matters by paying attention to the little things, including time management.

Like everything else, there are moments of success and ease when an entrepreneur tries to force several things that will ruin their business relationships. They run the constant risk of failing or being frustrated due to poor planning or organization when they are in charge of every aspect of their company.

What happens if time management isn't effective or yields the desired outcomes?

Is time management a problem for all online business owners?

Sometimes, remote business owners find that their processes and procedures aren't functioning. They find that no matter what they try, they are unable to stay focused and complete the necessary tasks or goals. They find that they are essentially ineffective time managers who are incapable of achieving either modest or large goals. Who else might be the offender? You're not managing your time well.

What consequences do those snares have? Does someone have good time management skills?

Acknowledging Your Current Level of Productivity

When it comes to your business, keep the following two things in mind, as they will have a significant impact on your production rate:

What's Taking Place Right Now

Starting the day without a plan of activity.

You're doomed from the get-go if you go into your day without a plan of action! You start out late and immediately feel in control. After that, you're on the defensive and in crisis mode much of the day.

Additionally, you could react hastily and arbitrarily to the problems and experiences of other people, putting their problems ahead of your own.

Absence of balance

In order to feel successful and successful, we need to practice equilibrium in seven important aspects of our lives:

Well-being is the state in which your body experiences and responds to external stimulation.

Family: spending time and taking care of loved ones.

Financial: the whole of tax obligations and fiscal burdens

Intellectual: The impact of outside stimulation on one's life

Social: the way you engage with others

Professionalism refers to the methods you use to easily progress your profession.

Spirituality is your connection to humans and the higher power.

Even while they can't all receive the same amount of time each day, each of those areas requires our daily attention to be complete. While it's important to spend some time in each area, it's not as important to devote a lot of time to each one.

Our lives will ultimately be harmonious and balanced if we invest enough time in each area, both in terms of quantity and quality. All of those areas are equal, and if we ignore any of them, we risk swiftly undermining our success.

For instance, our social lives and relationships with our loved ones deteriorate when we neglect our own well-being. Similarly, if our financial resources are out of balance, we won't be able to devote enough time to pursuing our ambitions of a successful job and other important areas of attention.

Cluttered Up Workspace

A disorganized workstation could lead to a disorganized mind.

Problems arise when you are unable to locate important business documents or client information. This junk not only creates chaos, confusion, and mayhem, but it can also result in missed payments and delayed invoices.

Research has shown that an individual working at a crowded desk spends one to two hours a day looking at or becoming sidetracked by items. This could result in a substantial weekly increase in wasted hours.

Bad sleep

Many online entrepreneurs blame inadequate sleep for their failure to meet targets or generate leads for their firms.

When it comes to important business operations, sleep deprivation can lead to illogical or bad decision-making.

Research has shown that almost 75% of internet firms suffer from sleep deprivation, which unintentionally affects their operations. A homemaker's productivity suffers when they are fatigued.

If the entrepreneur's lack of sleep doesn't have a detrimental effect on them, the quality of their sleep will. This implies that when they do sleep, it's usually a disturbed, fitful sleep brought on by underlying stress and other crippling factors.

For internet entrepreneurs, days loaded with stress are dangerous and should eventually turn negative. The secret is to get adequate sleep and rest so that you may feel less stressed and work more efficiently.

Refuse to Be Distracted

There is always a street that could divert you from your intended path on any given route. It may be a street with everything you want to see, everything you want to do to unwind, and everything that could encourage you to stray from your objective. So, avoid getting sidetracked. Avoid situations and moments such as these, as you may not be able to find your way back. You must be aware of who you are in order to avoid these things. Determine whether you have the strength to withstand the distractions and temptations. On your way to work, for instance, you might have passed a bookshop that had the book you were looking for. Then you asked yourself, "Should I ignore this or go in?"

It's acceptable to select option number one, which is to visit your favorite bookstore and read it. You were haggling with yourself, assuming that if you went inside, you would just glance at it and see how much it cost, not actually reading it. However, you also understood too well that you are prone to losing control. There's a good chance that if you go in, you'll read it, which would cause you to be late for work. You made the decision to keep going since your work took precedence over your book.

The lesson of time management is the same. Avoid being drawn away from your objective by distractions if you want to save time.

Staying on track is the last time management strategy you need to apply. To be more effective, you must maintain the habit of consistent time management. It's crucial to decide whether your approaches are worthwhile and sustainable before beginning anything. For instance, you've resolved to work twice a day in order to achieve your goal of being a millionaire by the age of thirty. You took action by working hard because you have previously determined your short-term goals and set the big picture. However, you stopped aiming for your objective at the age of 25 since you felt that it was not getting you any closer to it.

Another situation that can cause you to give up on your aspirations is if you've already run yourself into the ground before reaching your objective. Select an approach that you can easily stick to. The objective of completely giving up smoking is another illustration. You've made the decision to utilize a nicotine patch to help reduce your urges and smoking dependency. Don't use a nicotine patch if you believe the cost is too high, and you won't be able to stick with it. Consider another strategy to assist yourself in quitting. You can attempt using alternative remedies like acupressure, going to group therapy sessions, and other approaches.

Focus on One Task at a Time

People multitask most of the time in order to save time. However, many are unaware that rushing through tasks doesn't result in time savings. When anything is done quickly, it will not turn out well. Similar to a lady who watches TV while cooking and converses on the phone with her spouse, the food she is preparing burns. She would probably have to prepare another kilogram of pork again, which would be a waste of money and food in addition to time. As you can see, multitasking is not as beneficial as most people believe.

Give yourself something.

You must know when to stop and when to continue if you want to retain consistency in your time management. In the same way as the example given in the first section of the chapter, when you are trying to become wealthy by the age of thirty if you continue to work and save and work and save. Eventually, your brain and all of your senses will fail.

This is a result of your having used up all of your resources and running out of energy to carry on. Like a worker who puts in extra hours each day and then falls sick, she wouldn't be able to accomplish her goal on schedule because of an unforeseen circumstance.

That's why it's so important to relax. Effective time management is about using the least amount of time necessary to accomplish a goal without undue stress or weariness. It is not about achieving goals as quickly as feasible. Sickness undermines the goal of time management. To effectively manage your time, set, organize, and carry out your goals.

Using Hidden Time

All of us would adore having such extended periods of time to read and learn. There are moments when you truly do have those hours at your disposal. You might have a few hours at once to study if your timetable only allows you to attend classes three days a week and you don't have full-time or part-time employment during the rest of the week or children to take care of. You may have one or two hours at a time to read and study in between classes, even if your classes are spread out across four or five days. Well done! You're among the fortunate ones. You may find it difficult to avoid interruptions, both external and self-inflicted because you do have such large blocks of time. (For assistance in preventing distractions and maintaining concentration on your academic work, refer to the Chapter 7 section on Dealing with Interruptions.)

Nonetheless, there is a way to accomplish a lot, even if your schedule prevents you from having large blocks of time to complete your work, school, social, extracurricular, or family obligations. My term for it is "Making Use of Hidden Time." This is how you train yourself to be more productive, regardless of how long you have to read and study—15, 30, 45, 60, or more minutes at a time.

When someone looks at their busy schedule and says, "I just don't have time to read," or "I can't make the time to study with all my obligations," they can avoid the common pitfall by using this method.

Indeed, you can!

It doesn't matter if you read or study in short bursts—it still contributes to your overall short- or long-term objectives.

What are some strategies for making the most of your waiting periods? I'm not talking about checking your phone while operating a vehicle at all! It would be just as harmful as texting while driving, which is illegal in more than 40 states. Hopefully, all 50 states will enact legislation prohibiting texting and driving. In an emergency, it is legal in three states. The most obvious consequence of texting while driving is that it can cause distracted driving, which can result in accidents that are frequently fatal. If someone is injured or dies as a result of texting while driving, there may be legal repercussions that include summons, fines, or even arrest and jail time.

Ideas for Making the Most of College's Hidden Time

Establishing Beneficial Routines

Later, I spent a whole chapter on procrastination, a poor habit that far too many college students have developed and which undermines their ability to perform to the best of their abilities. This section focuses on creating constructive habits that will help you become a better time manager. A habit that has worked well for me is, for instance, reading or writing for at least an hour before I begin my day, regardless of whether it is spent teaching, doing research, or engaging in other professional or personal activities. Not only can I start the day with one or more of my top priorities completed, but it also gives me a sense of accomplishment while I tackle the other duties.

How do you usually start your day? Is there a way you could arrange your day or perhaps finish some schoolwork in the first thirty minutes or so after you wake up?

Is there another college-related pattern that you could establish or maintain if that one doesn't work for you because you would rather wake up, get ready, and just head out the door to work or classes? Maybe that could mean setting out at least two hours each night to read and study at the same time—before bed or after supper, for example?

Consider your days, nights, and even weekends during this time. Even if you already have routines that work well for you, or if you could use better ones, utilize this opportunity to reflect. Given your desire to perform to the best of your ability while attending college, what routines do you currently follow that are beneficial or detrimental? Where could you start one or more new practices that will improve your time management skills?

Putting Your Computer Files in Order

Searching through your Computer's storage for client projects, documents, invoices, emails, etc., may be a major time waster. Having so much hard drive space on your Computer is amazing, right? That is unless the item you're seeking is not found.

Here are a few tried-and-true suggestions for maintaining computer organization.

Think About Owning Two Computers

Regardless of whether you use a Mac or a Windows computer, think about owning two different machines. One can be used for personal purposes and the other for work. Your life will be so much simpler as a result. Additionally, there can be tax benefits as well, so make sure to speak with your accountant.

Another strategy to maintain focus and improve time management is to store your work files on a different PC. You won't have to spend time sorting through family photo files mixed in with corporate spreadsheets; instead, you'll be able to organize and locate crucial data much more quickly. Additionally, you should never, ever save sensitive customer data on a computer used for personal use.

Use Libraries to Organise Files in Windows 7 and 8

Have you ever seen your Windows computer's "libraries" section? Select Computer by clicking on your Start icon. The term LIBRARIES will appear on the left side of the window that appears.

In essence, you can keep various files in your library without having to relocate them from where they are. Windows comes with four libraries by default.

Videos Music Documents Images

It is also possible for you to add other folders of your own.

How to Utilise Libraries

First Step

Use Windows Explorer to navigate to Libraries (See above for instructions). Locate a folder containing our files that aren't already in your library. Anything that is presently stored on your desktop, for instance. To choose that file or folder, just click on it.

Step Two

You should now see an option to "Include in library" in the toolbar (above your file list) when you choose the folder or file as in step 1. From that list, you may now select one of your libraries. To view this example, simply select "Documents."

And that's it!

You will also find the option to "create new library" in the same window. You can set up distinct libraries for each area of your company. You won't have to waste time remembering where you put a particular file, which will save you a tonne of time. Rather, simply navigate to the relevant library folder and make a click.

Keep in mind that Windows doesn't relocate the original folder. Libraries simply create a second location, which makes finding files much faster.

How To Find Greater Passion In Your Life

Making a vĖsionboard, often referred to as a passionboard, can be extremely effective. This works especially well if you're a highly visual person. Making a pawnboard is really simple. Locate and highlight the words, symbols, and images that best capture the essence of each of your passions. Make a collage and only include an image if it truly conveys a powerful and intense emotion. Keep this somewhere that only you will see it. Locations that you frequently visit, like your bathroom or personal bedroom, are ideal for the majority of people.

Establish a Situation

A passion statement is not an absolute definition of what it means to be you or anyone else. Creating rules in your life or the lives of others is actually unnecessary unless, of course, this is your rule. Prevention is something that needs to be discovered rather than ruled into being.

Where do you now pursue your interests? Start crafting your passion statement on a 3' by 5' index card. It could be anything that makes sense to you at this time in your life, how you perceive the world, a goal to pursue, or how you feel about anything. For optimal outcomes, it is recommended that you edit and review these frequently, if feasible, even every day.

Consider Your Passions

Try writing your personal affirmations and/or favorite phrases on your own bathroom mirror using the same pen they use for whiteboards. These "dry erase" markers allow for simple cleaning when you're ready to modify or adjust your words. A good thing to use if you are unable to come up with words to write your personal statement. Every morning, as you brush your teeth and get ready for the day, read your power phrases. As you get ready for bed, read the mirror once more. Try experimenting with various color choices until your print looks both eye-catching and appealing.

Application Gratitude Principality

Passion abounds in places where gratitude prevails. When you are able or given the chance to accomplish anything, you naturally give it more love and care. Put your top five phrases on 3' x 5' index cards. Start by saying, "I'm so happy and grateful to be now" or "I'm so grateful now that..." and then list the top five things you are passionate about in life. Don't read them until they make you feel uncomfortable simply by thinking about them. Feel what it's like to have them. The dead write, "This orsomethinggreater now manifestsforthe good of all concerned." Place them strategically throughout your home or car, or carry them with you. Pull them out frequently, especially when you're feeling down or unappreciative.

Ensure Proper Sleep

Your sleep is perhaps the most significant aspect of your relationship with your partner. Exercise brings out the best in you, but it is impossible to function at your best if you are completely devoid of energy. You need the right amount of rest in order to be at your best. Have a strong desire to solve your sleep puzzle.

How long will it take you to acquire a consistent nighttime sleep pattern? Begin by experimenting with several items that seem to work. What could a warm bath, hot tea, earplugs, sleep mask, or music do for you? Start with small adjustments at a time. Modest alterations can significantly impact your total sleep quality.

Create a PAT Enabled Support Team

The people in your immediate vicinity have a greater influence on discovering and pursuing your passions than you may realize. One common mistake people make is attempting to discover their personal preferences on their own. Something that is intended to be shared and discovered with others is pardon. Locate and encircle yourself with like-minded and virtuous people. Make sure to reach out to those who have already successfully pursued their passions. Examine groups and associations, explore mentorship, or invest in a life coach. Your support team will provide objective and priceless guidance as required.

Put your imagination to use and be creative.

It comes naturally to conjure up ideas for all kinds of things all day long. Additionally, your mind processes an average of 70,000 thoughts per day. I would like to invite you to think about using one of those ideas as a chance to reflect on what meaningful living means to you. Perhaps it involves flying jeepneys in Thailand or managing several businesses globally. Perhaps it means working with researchers in the Cure Cancer Society or supporting the orphans in Africa.

Alternatively, it could signify spending each weekend with your closest friends and family. Remember back when you were younger? And the concepts appeared to be coherent. Remember when you were at liberty? The truth is that you are still the same person you were back then; it's just that your perspective on things has changed. Being creative is something that everyone naturally possesses; it's only a matter of regaining your innate creativity. Use your creativity!

Take Initiative to Restore the "Dream Stories" in Your Life

All ardent individuals surround themselves with other passionate, uplifted individuals. They opt to associate with individuals who either support or enhance their own being and act as a necessary complement to their lives. Someone who is content to just rain on everyone else's parade is known as a "Dream Squasher." They are quick to judge, fast to say no, and quick to seize opportunities. Those who truly mock the notion that you could have of purging your passion and creating your dreams. It is human nature to adapt to the environment in which one finds themselves, even with the best of intentions.

To-do lists as a means of reminding oneself of things that need to get done are not something I support. It appears that a lot of people utilize this technique to maximize their time. Lists, in my opinion, do not make things easier to do. Directly entering projects into a calendar and adding anticipated start and end times is a more efficient way to manage them. Using a digital task list is a helpful reminder if you need to build a list of things that need to be done but haven't been put on the calendar. To promote timely completion, include a completion date in either a handwritten or digital format.

Taking notes is also an effective way to capture brief reminders. When you're not in front of your computer, you can find yourself engaging in creative thinking, which frequently results in an increase in the amount of work that needs to be done. Make a list during these periods and give each project a deadline.

I still use a writing pad to take notes because I am that old-fashioned. This is merely a habit I picked up in elementary school. I personally find that writing things down on paper improves my memory, as shown by educational research. However, your tablet or smartphone can function just as well if you feel more at ease taking notes online. Again, it makes no difference what app you use to take notes. When you are unable to access the calendaring tool, choose a method that is convenient for you to write down chores that need to be completed.

Consider the places where you consider the greatest. Where do you generate the best ideas that you have? You might not be using your laptop or sitting in front of it at work. If so, you'll need to figure out a strategy to recall that idea in the future. I find that while I'm driving somewhere, I have the best ideas. That's not something you can write down or remember in that kind of situation. Frequently, by the time I arrive at my destination, the thought I was considering has slipped my mind. I bought a little voice recorder back in the days before smartphones to make sure I didn't forget what I was thinking. I would jot down a note to myself while I was driving, and when I got to my destination, I would update my task list. The same kind of recording functionality is now included in smartphones.

Now, think about the places where you think most clearly. How are you going to store those concepts for later?

Verify your calendar for today's activities related to sales and personal matters.

Examining your calendar to see today's work and personal schedule is the fourth stage in making a morning schedule. Do you have any tasks to complete before your client or prospect appointments this afternoon or this morning? If yes, put these chores right away on your to-do list and include any notes on the things you want to talk about with these customers.

Take into account the amount of time it will take to get from one sales meeting to the next when you look at your schedule of events and commitments.

Upon perusing the current meeting agenda and calendar, have you factored in sufficient time between your numerous sales appointments in case you need to wait at a customer's location? Has your schedule for today included any "buffer time"?

Next, see whether you have any back-to-back customer appointments scheduled for the day. Or are there any unoccupied time slots that you ought to attempt to occupy with spontaneous visits to other clients or potential clients? Lastly, is there anything going on after hours that you should know about and be ready for?

5. Sort through your "to-do" list each day.

You need to have been taking notes, making lists of things to do, and setting reminders on a daily to-do list (in a spiral notebook) while you went over, glanced over, and examined today's appointments and events.

Review everything you placed on your to-do list for today, including calls to make, emails to send, orders to write, activities to accomplish, and so forth, as the last step in your morning planning routine. Finally, assign a priority to each job on your list using the triage method. In the following two chapters, I'll go into further detail on triage.

Applying the "triage" structure of A, B, and C

The truth is that you might not be able to do everything on your daily job list if you have a tonne of other things to do in addition to having plenty of customers to call on. As part of your daily schedule, prioritize your to-do list each morning so you always know what needs to get done first and what can wait.

Setting a distinct priority for every job on your list is known as triaging. You can quickly determine which tasks have the highest priority for today by putting A, B, or C next to each one. This will also help you identify any tasks that may wait until tomorrow.

Writing down the chores, reminders, emails, and phone calls you want to get done today is the first step in making your daily to-do list every morning. Don't worry too much about the order in which you write your tasks down on your to-do list when you first start because triage will be applied when you're done. After you've listed the eight to ten goals you want to accomplish that day, return to the top of the list and, starting at the top and working your way down, put the letter A, B, or C next to each activity. This process is known as "triaging your list."

A = Take immediate action

Put an "A" next to the things on your daily to-do list that absolutely must be completed today. Before you do anything else, you have to finish these errands, emails, calls, or other chores. The tasks with an "A" next to them are essential to your sales position and must be completed today. When you mark a task on your list with an "A," you are informing yourself that there will be a bad outcome if it is not started or finished before the end of the day.

B = Do it better

Certain items on your list will not be "A" priorities; as a result, some will be significant but not urgent. Tasks "B" are what we'll call them. You should only perform these tasks after finishing the "A" tasks.

C = Capable of doing it

Put the letter "C" next to the tasks that still need to be completed. These will include some calls, emails, follow-ups, and other tasks that are your lowest priority for today and tomorrow but may become more important in a few days.

DISCLOSURE: Despite the fact that your list will include "C" items, resist the urge to start with them. Always begin by focusing on the most critical "A" tasks. This is so that your sales role will benefit most from "A" assignments.

Throughout the day, don't forget to refer to your to-do list—ideally, it's in your spiral notebook. Check your list frequently, and when you finish chores, send and receive emails, and make phone calls, make sure to check them off so you can concentrate on the remaining activities and tasks.

2. Do you prefer paper or electronic media?

Whatever calendar or journaling app you choose, keep in mind that it needs to be:

Simple to bring to client meetings.

Prepared for usage while you're in your car (recording appointment notes).

When it's back in your office on your desk, it's easy to use and retrieve.

In my experience, while some of those enormous paper-based time management diary systems may seem impressive, their mass and girth make them difficult to tote around all day. All things considered, you will need to select a portable diary and calendar—either paper or electronic—that complement your kind of sales role and way of life.

Let me provide one additional observation regarding the use of diaries and calendars. It's crucial to keep up appearances if you sell to big corporate clients and meet mostly with senior management. When taking notes during your sales meetings, you should utilize a high-quality pen, a spiral notebook housed in a leather compendium, and an upscale diary. I promise you that senior executives will notice these items, notably your pen when you are having sales meetings with them.

As a general rule, the price and exclusivity of the goods or services you offer should directly relate to the caliber of your journal, compendium, pen, and other accessories. For instance, you may get away with using a cheap pen and diary if your business is selling nuts and bolts. However, if you offer pricey, high-end consulting services, you'll need to utilize a high-quality notebook with a leather cover and pull out a Mont Blanc pen or something like that.

For example, if you sell IT solutions, you might want to take notes during meetings using something like the newest 12.9-inch iPad Pro with the Apple Bluetooth Pen that comes with it.

Visitors Who Drop By

As you labor feverishly on a pressing assignment that is running out of time, you hear someone ask, "Do you have a minute?" Have these inquiries consistently dragged on for more than a minute after you kindly replied, "Yes?" This can take away from your productive time and is highly prevalent.

It's possible that coworkers will prevent you from completing your task on time if they drop by your office for just "one minute." Your productivity can significantly decrease if this "one minute" of your time requests takes up your entire day. When someone asks for a minute of your time, they may rapidly find themselves at ease in your company and begin talking about topics unrelated to their initial request.

It is crucial to plan time for uninterrupted work, even though some organizations follow the "open-door policy," or you might not be lucky enough to have a private office with a door that can be closed. There is no other method to finish the things that you have prioritized. Try putting some of the following advice to use to stop unplanned "drop-in" visitors from squandering your valuable time:

Rearrange your desk such that the traffic outside your office faces away from you. Eye contact of any kind can result in unexpected disruptions.

Any office supplies that must be used frequently by others, including common files, should be moved from your workplace to a general office area.

Make time in your daily calendar for priorities each day, and try your best to stick to it. Prior to receiving email in the morning, work on big, significant projects or activities to avoid interruptions. Establishing a quiet moment during the day for yourself is equally important. Eat your lunch away from your work, or otherwise, people will think you're constantly available.

Inform your colleagues that you will only take meetings after a specific time in the morning if you are not available before then.

Plan out the times when you will be unavailable and honor that timetable.

Shut your door and separate yourself if you have an office. A "do not disturb" sign can even be something you consider hanging on your door. If you don't have an office, try working in solitude in a conference room.

If you can, think about working from home on certain workdays. You'll be shocked at how much more productive you can be when you have undisturbed time at home as opposed to at work.

You are not required to maintain an open-door policy. This merely transfers your power—that is, the ability to control your time—to others. An open-door policy really only means that you're usually reachable by phone or email when time allows. This guideline does not imply that you are available to people at all times.

Ask your helper to help you manage your time if you have one. Establish explicit rules about the times you are and are not available for meetings. Make sure your assistant arranges your meetings on the same day as you work.

In situations where engaging with an individual is unavoidable, particularly in cases of urgency, collect relevant information and take quick action or reschedule the encounter for a later time of day. Make sure you are aware of how long this will take.

In the event that someone requests a brief period of your attention or wishes to meet with you later in the day, tell them to make an appointment.

If coworkers are constantly interrupting you, ask them to gather all the information they need to discuss with you and set up an afternoon time to go over everything at once. This is a great way to reduce interruptions and save time.

If someone comes into your office wanting to "talk stories," urge them to summarise the situation while you are working on a crucial assignment.

If your office has chairs, place objects like your briefcase on the chairs to deter people from sitting and engaging in lengthy conversations with you. Some find empty chairs to be highly enticing.

Try using some of these suggestions if there are people who will not accept the fact that you need to set up a meeting or that you are preoccupied with a project. For certain people, it may seem impolite, but it is necessary:

Make up a meeting that requires you to depart.

Tell them you have to make an important phone call about an urgent matter. This might put an end to the current discussion.

Give the discussion a time limit. Make sure to clearly indicate when the allotted time has passed and that you need to return to your work.

Attack Your Day! Author Mark Woods Prior to It Attacking You: Rule of Activities Interruptions are employed with a color-coding scheme by Not the Clock. This serves as a manual for handling the four primary categories of workplace disruptions. Red, green, yellow, and grey codes are used to identify the disruptions.

You can handle constant disruptions with the aid of this color system, allowing you to be more productive in your work. Consider the color that this is related to.

Red: A critical and urgent issue. This is something that must be taken care of right now. At this point, you should put your work on hold and take immediate action to handle the pressing issue.

Green: Although the disruption might not be an emergency, it still has to be addressed right away and not put off.

Yellow: There is no need to respond to this interruption right away. Something needs to get done, but it can wait until later in the day or the following day.

Grey: These are the time-wasting disruptions that are wholly unnecessary. This is deserving of merely a "no."

Make sure that your strategies don't negatively impact the atmosphere within your company. You don't want the general atmosphere at work and any standard procedures to be compromised by your benefits. There are situations when you have to isolate yourself in order to do your work. You have to be mindful of your time and deadlines, even though it can irritate certain people. They can waste their time as they choose, but not yours.

monetary institution

Your monthly budget will be created much more easily if your finances and related papers and files are organized. This will be covered in full in the upcoming chapter. You should concentrate on organizing all of your documentation for the time being. Being organized is crucial since, should you lose sight of your unpaid invoices, you may be hit with unanticipated financial consequences such as interest and late fees. It's likely not necessary for you to implement every recommendation in this section in order to manage your money. To create a functional system that efficiently arranges your finances, I advise you to select the suggestions that are relevant to your particular circumstance.

Keep up with your bills first. Every day, gather the items in your mailbox. Open any bill that comes in the mail as soon as you receive it. Even though seeing the amount that is still due on your statement may not be pleasant, putting it off won't help you. Then, pay the bill right away if you have the funds to do so. At that point, you can cross that bill off your tangible or mental to-do list of financial obligations and move on.

Likewise, maintain your bill file by creating a three-column bill list. This is not to be mistaken with the budget with three columns that we shall talk about in the following chapter. Put all of the invoices you anticipate receiving in a given month in the column on the far left of your bills list. Just write the names of the bills themselves, such as "utilities" or "auto insurance," and don't worry too much about the amount you anticipate seeing on that bill for the time being. Next, list the names of the bills you receive in the middle column, followed by the dates on which you receive each one and its associated due date. Lastly, enter the name of each bill and the date of payment submission in the third column as soon as you have paid it. You will have your list as a reference if you and a business or creditor disagreeabout one of your debts. Additionally, you won't be left wondering if, for example, you still need to set aside money for your credit card bill.

The next thing you'll need is a stack of bills and costs that is physically ordered. Organize all of your bills in one location. Maybe you put something away in a file cabinet, a desk drawer, or a level on a stacking tray. Either way, having all of your bills in one physical place will save you from having to search everywhere for a specific bill's data when you need it. If you receive your bills electronically, arrange them all into a single email or file folder. Subdirectories are also perfectly acceptable as long as you have a single master folder that contains all of them. In a similar vein, you have the liberty to separate or group your hard-copy invoices within their primary directory.

If you enjoy using technology, you might want to use specialized financial software. Numerous financial software programs are made to assist users in managing their personal finances. A basic Excel spreadsheet can also assist most people in maintaining their financial organization.

To improve their financial organization, some financial gurus advise opening two checking accounts. They recommend keeping one account for basic expenses and another for luxuries. Your goal should be to maintain a balance in your necessary spending account that is sufficient to pay for all of your monthly required costs. For amusement, you have another account. For instance, keeping a second account for discretionary spending can assist you in avoiding using your energy bill money to purchase booze when you go out for drinks with friends. It is advised that you keep the debit card linked to your checking account for essential purchases within your house. In order to use that card to pay their bills online, some people even go so far as to tear it apart, leaving only the digits intact.

The necessity to maintain organization increases if you share an account with a spouse, partner, or other family member. You are accountable not only for your personal budgeting, saving, and spending practices but also for those of others. You run the risk of unintentionally overdrafting the account if you don't know how much the other person associated with it has spent. It is important for joint account owners to keep in regular contact with one another about account-related financial matters. Additionally, it is imperative that you two confer before one of you makes a significant purchase.

Also, those who have signed up for direct deposit should make sure that their paychecks consistently reach the associated account on schedule. Check the balance on the associated account as soon as you anticipate receiving your directly deposited paycheck to make sure you don't inadvertently spend more than you have available. In spite of the fact that your next salary is still a ways off, doing this could result in overdraft costs. It is not unusual for incoming funds to be placed on hold while the bank confirms its authenticity. You might be able to save worry and waste money by quickly checking your balance each payday.

After creating your budget, you should consult it before making any significant financial decisions. While the next chapter's budget plan is designed to help users navigate their financial circumstances month-to-month, you should be reviewing it more often than once every thirty days. You will need to update your budget on a regular basis and make any required adjustments if you want to keep it organised.

And lastly, save whatever financial documentation you get. Have them arranged in one location. Save all of your receipts, pay stubs, bills, IOUs, and other records that show your revenues and expenses.

Boost Your Understanding

It's time to start learning more about your niche now that you have identified it. You should have chosen a topic you are well-versed in if you answered the questions above correctly. You probably don't know everything there is to know about your niche, despite the fact that you may believe you do. Since things are constantly changing, it's critical to have as much knowledge as you can.

This does not obligate you to attend classes or pay for tuition. And conducting internet research on your niche. You can accelerate your learning process by expanding your general knowledge in a few other ways as well.

Intelligence in general

Like all the other muscles in your body, the brain needs to be worked out. You will improve as a learner, thinker, and focused individual if you exercise your brain as much as possible and in the appropriate ways. Your capacity to learn and think clearly will start to decline if you choose not to use your brain and instead injure it with harmful objects.

Here are five strategies to improve the power and efficiency of your brain:

Reduce how much TV you watch.

People find it difficult to do this. The majority of people's favorite past time is to veg out in front of the television. The issue with TV is that it prevents your brain from functioning or recovering. After watching TV for a few hours straight, don't you find that you're exhausted? Red, painful, and dry eyes from staring at the screen.

Pick up a book and read to unwind. Perhaps you would prefer to listen to music than read. Make the decision to converse with others when you're with them rather than watching TV. Your mind will be stimulated more by these activities than by watching TV.

Work It Out

You might believe that you would learn more if you decided to read a book rather than exercise. Not always. Your learning will be enhanced by the time you spend exercising because you'll be more productive afterward. You will get energy and be able to think more clearly after working out. You'll have more energy and be able to focus better.

Read books that are difficult.

Popular books, such as suspense fiction, are enjoyable to read for most people, but they don't usually make you think. Go through books that require concentration to help you write and think more clearly. A classic novel will alter your perspective on the world, so it's a wise choice. If you need to look up a few words, that's okay. The dense reading shouldn't scare you. You'll become accustomed to the author's writing style if you take your time and reread anything.

Make sure you get enough rest.

If you get the chance, try to nap for no longer than twenty minutes during the day. If you were to experience a wave of drowsiness, this would help you overcome it. You're probably going to wake up feeling exhausted if your nap lasts longer than 20 minutes.

Think back

It's possible for life to get busy, and you won't even recognize it. Your thoughts will make it more difficult for you to focus. Make sure you set aside some time for introspection, thought organization, and responsibility alignment. You will know what matters most after you have had time to reflect. Anything insignificant won't get to you.

Though they might not seem like much, these suggestions will improve your ability to concentrate and learn, allowing you to process as much information as possible. Now that you have a general understanding of learning tips let's look at some methods for researching information specific to your niche.

Acquiring knowledge

The majority of that information is freely available for use. This implies that you have no excuse for not being able to gain as much knowledge and insight into your niche as possible.

Go through:

Reading up on your niche is the simplest thing you can do. These could be books or internet articles. Find some books, articles, and websites that are related to your niche by starting your research.

Locate Books:

Look for books in your area of interest. You'll learn the most from those that you find interesting. Purchasing a book copy to keep for eternity is the best option. To see if you can find a free copy of the book, you can also try searching on websites like Project Gutenberg.

Audiobooks:

Audiobooks are probably best for you if you're not a reader or if you don't like eBooks. Most books are available as audiobooks. After locating the book using the previous step, try to locate its audio version. In this manner, the book can be listened to in the car or while working.

Soundtrack:

If music isn't your niche, this one won't teach you anything about it, but it can aid with concentration. Listening to jazz or classical music while working can boost your intelligence and create a relaxing atmosphere. You can find many free places to listen to this music online. Playing this while you read or work on your niche is a good idea.

Online Courses:

These days, a lot of colleges and universities provide free course materials online in the form of podcasts or notes. Finding information and classes related to your niche shouldn't be too difficult if you do a little research. Additionally, there are websites like Coursera that provide millions of online courses along with a loan-free financial aid option.

Teaching Videos:

Similar to what was mentioned above, some colleges are making their lectures available to view online for free. Look through video-sharing websites such as YouTube to find these kinds of videos.

E-mail Correspondence Course:

There are plenty of classes that you can have sent to you through your e-mail. You can receive a course on just about any subject, so you shouldn't have a problem finding something about your niche.

Before you can become an expert in your niche, you have to learn as much as possible. Start using some of the above suggestions for expanding your intelligence and knowledge today. If you are invested in your niche, then researching and learning about it won't seem that hard or like a chore.

The Time Management Matrix Of Stephen Covey

Framework for Time Control

We all have the same 24 hours a day, even when it seems like time is rushing out. And why are certain people ready to go above and beyond what the majority of people are willing to accomplish? Their ability to manage resources better than others points to another possible explanation. However, how do we handle the deluge of tasks that all require our immediate attention? The Covey Time Management System will assist you in managing the limited time more skillfully when meeting deadlines is a necessity. More than ever, the Covey matrix helps you organize your goals. Using four distinct quadrants,

The matrix, which is also known as Eisenhower's Urgent-Significant Concept, makes a distinction between significance and urgency by stating that vital tasks are related to achieving the objectives.

Urgent tasks require prompt attention. These actions also have a direct bearing on someone else's goal being accomplished. Neglecting these issues could lead to dire consequences.

Here's a summary of each quadrant's meaning:

Quadrant I: Extremely important deadlines Urgently needed tasks and activities are included in the first quadrant.

Long-term planning and policy in Quadrant II For problems where immediate action is not required, the second quadrant is crucial. Covey notes that a long-term plan might make use of this quadrant.

High-urgency distractions in Quadrant III Activities that are urgent but unrelated are placed in the third quadrant. Reducing or eliminating such situations is advised by Covey, as they don't improve your performance. Here, delegation is an additional option.

Quadrant IV: Operations of little to no significance The final and fourth quadrant is devoted to meaningless tasks and activities, or those that are neither urgent nor crucial. Avoiding such time-wasters is crucial.

A large portion of your tasks will fall into Quadrants I and III when you use the Covey Time Management Model in your own personal and private life.

Experience shows that most people miss Quadrant II, particularly when it comes to their own personal development.

All the same, one cannot undervalue the second quadrant. A significant divergence in this quadrant suggests that the strategic perspective is being neglected and that the tactical side is being heavily weighted. Covey is talking about quadrant II as an extremely important part of the matrix for this purpose. There will be no efficient time control in this area.

Covey's time management matrix is explained.

The Covey Time Management Matrix The Covey Time Management Matrix below provides a detailed explanation of each of the four quadrants.

Immediate and Significant (Quadrant 1)

One can distinguish the jobs in Quadrant 1 from those that were not foreseeable. By formulating suggestions and closely monitoring their implementation, the aforementioned can be prevented. The only jobs and responsibilities in the first quadrant are those that require your complete focus. The space is set aside for emergency scenarios and pressing deadlines. In the event of a major issue, you will need to postpone some activities.

Quadrant 2: Not urgent, but crucial

Items in Quadrant 2 are not given much importance, even though they can be crucial later on. This quadrant is assigned to job problems, employment, fitness, and well-being, in addition to strategic strategies. It may not be required to invest resources in these areas at this time. To prevent quadrant two chores from becoming quadrant one objects, it would be quite important to carefully consider if you have allotted enough time for them in the long run. This will make it easier for you to turn in your assignments on time.

Quadrant 3: Important but not noteworthy

Things that appear to be very important but are, in fact not necessary are included in the third quadrant. Any of these actions could be meaningless and entirely motivated by ego. These things are actually obstacles that get in the way of your goals. If required, try assigning specific instances or suggest rescheduling them. If someone else is bothering you in Quadrant 3, you might be able to politely decline their request. If you are unable to make this decision, try not to become constantly sidetracked by giving timestamps to those who also need your assistance. This approach will resolve all of their problems simultaneously and won't take away from your everyday concentration.

Quadrant 4: Not important nor noteworthy

The items that don't offer any interest at all—the seeming time losses—are all included in the fourth and final quadrant. Every incident within is merely a diversion; try your hardest to put an end to it. No matter how humorous something appears in this chart, you will always try to remove it.

Utilizing the Time Matrix

It is recommended that you try to maximize the amount of time you spend on Quadrant II jobs while using the Important-Urgent array. In the long run, this would lead you to downplay the activities in Quadrant I because many of them could have been in Quadrant II if appropriate planning had been done.

If so, these tasks should take precedence over other things that require your attention but might not help you achieve your goals. Postpone activities that don't result in significant output until after more important initiatives are finished.

There are numerous uses for Covey's Time Management Grid; two of these will be discussed below.

Reordering the items on your existing "to-do" list

You can use the time matrix as a tool to rearrange the order of significance and urgency for both upcoming and ongoing tasks. You will be able to categorize tasks that need your urgent attention more quickly if you put chores and commitments into the proper order.

A week-long assessment

A weekly review is the second option for using the time management strategy. Six blank copies of the chart are needed: one for your weekly appraisal and five for each working day. You include all of your responsibilities, the time you spent on each, and the conclusion of each workday. You'll have created a single chart that summarises the five days of the week by the conclusion of the week. Make sure you specify how much time is spent on each mission. You will evaluate how well the time has been spent and decide whether or not to make any changes after summarising the week.

Observation and Modification

Finally, keep in mind how crucial it is to keep an eye on your time management process and modify your techniques as needed.

Maintain a monitoring diary in which you can log your everyday actions, assess your progress, and modify your strategies as necessary.

This will support sustained growth, motivation, and attention.

It is imperative that you make a commitment to implementing the ideas and tactics discussed in this chapter into your everyday life.

Recall that persistence and practice are necessary for efficient time management.

Here are some examples of how to apply what you've learned:

Decide to dedicate yourself to: Decide to focus on increasing your personal efficiency and managing your time better.

Although it will require work, the rewards will be worthwhile.

Implement the improvement objectives: Referring back to the improvement objectives you established in this chapter, begin their implementation.

Keep in mind that every goal needs to be tackled progressively and realistically.

Begin with minor adjustments, then move on to more difficult tasks as your confidence grows.

Make a plan of action: Create a precise and well-defined action plan for every improvement goal.

Put the actions you must conduct, the materials you require, and the due dates you have established in writing.

Remember that having a well-organized plan will assist you in staying on course.

Track your development: Monitor your progress towards set targets on a regular basis.

Celebrate your progress along the way and make modifications as necessary.

You may maintain your motivation and focus by continuously monitoring.

Seek advice and assistance: Take into consideration getting help from a coach, mentor, or support group on the outside.

They can offer insightful advice, direction, and extra inspiration.

Sharing your path with others can also inspire and benefit from mutual learning.

Recall that time management is a continuous process of self-development.

Be willing to try new things, adjust to new situations, and take lessons from your mistakes and accomplishments.

Creating a strong time management plan starts with a thorough personal assessment.

We'll look at goal-setting and prioritisation techniques, action plan creation, and practice implementation in the upcoming chapters to help you become a more proficient time manager.

I have no doubt that the things you do will pay off for you.

Recognising Time Wasters

One of the most important steps in evaluating your current time utilization and improving your time management skills is identifying time wasters. Activities that take up a lot of time yet don't advance your objectives or general well-being are called time wasters. Making the most of your time and achieving your objectives can be facilitated by recognizing and minimizing or doing away with certain activities. The following advice can be used to spot time wasters:

1. Understand the distinction between activities that are productive and those that are not: It's critical to comprehend the distinction between productive and non-productive tasks before you can spot time wasters. While non-productive activities don't offer value or are

harmful to your goals or well-being, productive activities support your goals, personal development, or overall well-being.

2. Keep track of your time: This is a useful tool for figuring out who is wasting time. After a week or two, make a note of your activities and classify them as productive, non-productive, or neutral. Examine your findings to determine which activities take up the most time and don't advance your objectives or general well-being.

3. Look for trends: You can identify time wasters by noticing patterns in the way you use your time. For instance, it's probably a waste of time if you spend hours every day reading through social media. Examine your time usage patterns to identify trends, such as days of the week or times of day when you tend to spend more time on unproductive activities.

4. Assess your habits: You might find time wasters by assessing your habits.

For instance, this might be a major time waster if you have a tendency to put off crucial duties. Analyze your routines and note any that are detrimental to your well-being or your goals.

5. Take the opportunity cost into account: When determining time wasters, take the opportunity cost of participating in unproductive activities into account. Opportunity cost is the expense of forgoing a choice in favor of following a particular path of action. For example, you are sacrificing the opportunity to accomplish something more meaningful or satisfying if you spend hours watching TV.

Examining Activities That Are Productive And Non-Productive

A critical component of efficient time management is analyzing activities that are productive and non-productive. Identifying the activities that provide value or are harmful to your goals or wellbeing (non-productive activities) and those that do not is the first step in this process of determining whether activities contribute to your goals, personal progress, or wellbeing (productive activities). When examining productive and non-productive actions, keep the following in mind:

1. Distinguish between actions that are productive and ineffective: It's critical to recognize the distinction between productive and ineffective actions. Engaging in activities that advance your

personal development, enhance your quality of life, and assist you in reaching your objectives is considered productive. Conversely, non-productive activities are those that squander your time, divert your attention from your objectives, or harm your general well-being wellbeing.

2. Evaluate the effects of your activities: Take into account how your activities affect your life when you analyze them. For instance, spending hours on social media scrolling may not be beneficial to your wellbeing or aspirations. Rather, it could divert your attention from other important pursuits that advance your well-being, wellbeing or personal development.

3. Assess your priorities: Part of analyzing your activities, both productive and non-productive, is assessing your priorities. Decide which

activities are most important to you and which fit in with your objectives and values. Give these tasks top priority and give them additional time. Conversely, determine which activities are ineffective and unnecessary for your life, then cut them out of your schedule.

4. Take into account the opportunity cost: When evaluating your actions, take into account the opportunity cost of doing unproductive things. Opportunity cost is the price of giving up a choice in order to follow a particular course of action. For instance, you are losing out on opportunities to partake in more fruitful or satisfying activities if you spend hours watching TV.

5. Be truthful with yourself: You must be sincere with yourself if you want to analyze your actions successfully. This entails identifying pursuits that can be time-wasting or detracting from your

objectives. It also entails being open to modifying your schedule and getting rid of unproductive pursuits that don't advance your well-being and wellbeing.

In conclusion, one of the most important aspects of efficient time management is the analysis of productive and non-productive tasks. You may choose how to spend your time more wisely if you take these tactics into account. This can support your personal development and wellbeing, help you reach your goals, and make your life more meaningful.

If at all possible, save the vacuuming and mopping for the weekends.

When feasible, scheduling your vacuuming and mopping for the weekends can be a wise move that will help single mothers a lot. Single mothers frequently balance jobs, child care, and other commitments during the workday, which leaves them with little time and energy.

These more time-consuming housekeeping chores can wait until the weekend, giving single mothers valuable weeknight evenings to spend with their kids, taking care of themselves, or just relaxing.

This method also guarantees that the house stays reasonably clean throughout the week, which lessens the strain of having to keep everything immaculate every day.

Furthermore, involving kids in weekend cleaning tasks can be a great way to instill in them a sense of accountability and cooperation.

Ultimately, single parents may balance keeping their home tidy and spending quality time with their kids throughout the week by saving up the mopping and vacuuming for the weekends.

As you proceed, especially in the kitchen, clean.

For single mothers, cleaning as you go is an invaluable practice that may greatly simplify their everyday lives, especially in the kitchen. The kitchen, which is frequently the center of a house, can easily get cluttered and disorganized when food is prepared and cooked in it.

Single mothers can lessen the stress of waking up to a pile of dirty dishes and counters after supper by cleaning as they go. This keeps the kitchen neat and orderly throughout the day.

In addition to increasing slips and accidents brought on by spilled liquids or food particles, this technique also increased safety.

Additionally, it saves time over time because less thorough cleaning is needed at the end of the day. Keeping a clean and well-functioning kitchen can significantly improve the daily routine and general wellbeing of single mothers who are already juggling a lot of duties.

To organize different household objects, utilize baskets.

For a number of reasons, using baskets to gather and arrange different objects in a single mother's home is a useful and effective tactic.

Primarily, it fosters neatness and organization, which is essential in a household where time and energy are sometimes few.

Toys, clothes, knickknacks, and electronics all have their own special place in a basket, which reduces clutter and makes finding objects easier.

Children who utilize this method also learn the importance of responsibility and organization as they are taught to put things back in their assigned baskets after use. Also, it saves time because single mothers won't have to spend it looking for lost objects all the time.

In addition, baskets are available in a variety of shapes and sizes, so single mothers can match them to their interior design scheme for a stylish and useful solution.

All things considered, using baskets for organization is a straightforward but efficient technique for single mothers to keep their homes stress-free and organized.

Handle dryer sheets in a baseboard manner.

For single mothers who want to keep their homes tidy and comfortable, rubbing dryer sheets around the baseboards is a smart and practical tip.

Baseboards might take a long time to clean since they frequently gather dust and grime over time. Single mothers can efficiently remove dust and grime and leave behind a nice and fresh aroma by using dryer sheets.

This keeps the interior of the house smelling better and looking cleaner, making it feel cozier and more welcoming.

This quick and simple procedure may also be completed in spare time, which makes it a practical option to maintain household cleaning schedules without investing a lot of time and energy.

It's an easy yet powerful method to improve the general ambiance and cleanliness of the house, which can be crucial for single mothers juggling hectic schedules and a lot of duties.

Establish a capsule wardrobe for your kids and yourself.

One clever, useful way to help single mothers and their kids simplify their lives is to make a capsule wardrobe for each of them. Time limits and the need for efficiency in household management are common challenges faced by single mothers. They can expedite the daily process of getting dressed by creating a capsule wardrobe.

For mothers, this means lowering the stress of daily decision-making by having a variety of adaptable, mix-and-match clothes items that are appropriate for different occasions.

A capsule wardrobe makes sure kids have an easy-to-manage collection of well-fitting, easily coordinated clothes, which makes getting dressed in the mornings easier and helps them learn the value of consuming less.

Additionally, by encouraging mothers and children to invest in well-made, long-lasting apparel, capsule wardrobes encourage conscious and sustainable buying. Long-term cost savings are also achieved by this strategy by lowering the requirement for frequent clothes purchases.

All things considered, a capsule wardrobe can ease some of the difficulties single mothers encounter in running their homes, freeing them up to concentrate on more significant facets of family life.

To save drying time, use a wool ball in the dryer.

Due to their hectic schedules, single mothers need to be as efficient as possible with their everyday responsibilities. One minor adjustment that might have a large impact on their laundry routine is using wool balls in the dryer.

Wool dryer balls facilitate faster drying times by distributing moisture and improving the flow of hot air between garments. In the long run, this lowers utility expenses because it saves time and energy.

Wool dryer balls are also safer for the family's health and the environment because they are a natural and environmentally friendly substitute for dryer sheets that are loaded with chemicals.

The ease of use and efficiency of this laundry hack will be appreciated by single mothers, who can use the time and money saved to focus on other important duties and quality time with their kids.

What makes time management techniques crucial?

For many reasons, time management techniques are vital in our daily lives. We can enhance our emotional health, raise our productivity, and eventually improve the quality of our lives by comprehending and putting these strategies into practice. Here, we go into great detail about the significance of these tactics.

To begin with, effective time management raises production and efficiency. With so many things to do and information to take in in today's fast-paced world, it's natural to feel overburdened. Time eludes us like water, and most of the time, we feel like we haven't accomplished everything we set out to accomplish. By prioritizing and organizing our tasks, time management tactics enable us to do more in less time. These tactics include goal-setting and planning procedures, as well as methods for focusing and removing distractions.

Time management also helps us achieve a better work-life balance. Making efficient use of our time enables us to keep our personal and professional obligations apart, preventing one from invading the other. Knowing when to work and when to relax, commit ourselves to our loved ones and take time for ourselves are all important. This sharp division between the various facets of our existence contributes to a decrease in stress and an increase in job and personal happiness.

Third, being proactive rather than reactive is made possible by effective time management. If we don't plan ahead, we can discover that most of what we do is a reaction to what is going on in the world. By putting time management techniques into practice, we can take control and focus our efforts on the objectives that truly matter. We can take control of our own circumstances in this way rather than just reacting to external ones.

Furthermore, time management skills enhance our capacity for decision-making. Our decisions can be hurried and less wise when we are under duress. We can lessen this strain and give ourselves time to think things through and come to wise judgments by managing our time.

Finally, effective time management has been linked to improved mental health. We may prevent work overload and reduce stress by implementing time management techniques, which improves our mental health.

To put it briefly, time management techniques are essential to our daily existence. They enhance our emotional health and sense of fulfillment in life in addition to making us more effective and productive. We can have more satisfying and balanced lives if we embrace and put these strategies into practice.

Maintain a Time diary: To begin, begin by keeping a thorough time diary for at least one week. Keep a record of everything you do, no matter how minor or unimportant it may seem. Make accurate and truthful entries. This will provide you with an overview of your entire time management.

Examine Your Time Record: Go over the entries you made in your time record and group your activities. Work-related duties, personal activities, leisure, and distractions are examples of common categories. Particular attention should be paid to tasks that occupy a large amount of your day.

Seek Out Trends: Examine your time log to find any reoccurring patterns or trends. Are there any particular tasks that always take longer than you anticipated? Do you observe time wasted on pointless chores or a lot of interruptions?

Evaluate Your Level of Productivity: Consider how productive you were at different tasks. Do you have periods of great productivity and periods of low productivity? Make an effort to identify the elements influencing your productivity—or lack thereof.

Analyse Your Digital Habits: Screen time can be a major time waster in the modern digital world. Examine your usage of computers and other digital devices, such as cell phones. Make a note of the websites, applications, and social networking sites you use most frequently.

Think About Your Own Habits: Consider your own routines and behaviors. Are there any time-wasting habits that you can think of, such as excessive perfectionism, disorganization, or procrastination? You can deal with these tendencies by recognizing them.

Track Abruptions: Throughout the day, be aware of any disruptions in your personal and professional life. Make a note of whether these disruptions can be avoided or are required. You can better handle interruptions if you can identify their causes.

Evaluate Emails and Meetings: Look at how much time is spent on emails, meetings, and communication. Exist any meetings that could be streamlined or canceled? Do you find yourself using email excessively or communicating needlessly?

Examine Your Recreational Activities: Even while leisure time is necessary for relaxation, spending too much time on it might be a waste of time. Examine your free time activities to see if they support your values and overarching goals.

Request Feedback: Other people's opinions might occasionally offer insightful analysis of your time wasters. Find out if your family, friends, or coworkers have observed any patterns in your time management that you may work on.

Set Task Priorities: Review how you prioritized your tasks. Do you find yourself putting off high-priority duties in favor of low-priority ones? Adapt your list of priorities to the significance and immediacy of each assignment.

Try Out Some Time Management Strategies: Experiment with various time management approaches and ideas to determine which ones assist you in overcoming particular time wasters. Task batching, the Pomodoro Technique, and time blocking are a few examples of useful techniques.

It takes self-awareness, introspection, and a desire to adjust routines and habits to recognize your time wasters. You may use your time more effectively and productively by taking action to reduce or eliminate these time wasters once you've discovered them.

The desire to give in to our instincts is one of the largest obstacles we encounter when attempting to accomplish our goals. We might have unhealthy food cravings, skipping workouts, or refraining from self-care. We can withstand these temptations and stay true to our plan when we have discipline. There may probably be times when we feel doubtful and discouraged because this is not always easy. However, we can overcome these obstacles if we keep in mind our objective and the strides we have already accomplished.

Consistency is another essential component of discipline when it comes to taking care of our bodies. The capacity for long-term discipline maintenance is known as consistency. It demands that we maintain our motivation and attention even in the face of setbacks or poor progress. Achieving our goals requires consistency because it enables us to advance steadily over time.

An essential idea in several disciplines, such as computer science, physics, and mathematics, is consistency. Generally speaking, consistency is the quality of a system or set of rules that guarantees the same results or outcomes regardless of the particular input or starting conditions.

The quality of a collection of axioms that guarantees that no contradictions can be deduced from them is known as consistency in mathematics.

The quality of a physical theory that guarantees that its predictions coincide with experimental findings is referred to as consistency in physics. For instance, because multiple tests have verified its predictions, the theory of relativity is regarded as consistent with experimental findings.

The quality of a system or algorithm that guarantees that its outputs are the same, independent of the particular input or initial conditions, is referred to as consistency in computer science. A consistent sorting algorithm would be one that consistently yields the same result for the same input, for instance.

Consistency is also a key idea. Consistency in various domains describes an individual's long-term consistent behavior or mental habits. One is said to be consistent in behavior, for instance, if they constantly act with honesty and integrity.

In the business sector, consistency is crucial, particularly when it comes to customer service. Businesses with a strong customer service record have a higher chance of gaining new clients as well as keeping existing ones. Maintaining consistency in product quality is crucial for businesses as it fosters customer trust and loyalty.

All things considered, consistency is an important idea in many facets of life. In any field—mathematics, physics, computer science, psychology, or business—consistency promotes order and predictability in the outside world and guarantees that outcomes are predictable and trustworthy.

It's also crucial to remember that consistency, which is the degree to which a person's behavior remains constant and predictable across time and in many contexts, is also known as a feature in personality psychology. Because it is linked to duty, dependability, and reliability, this trait is typically seen as favorable.

To sum up, consistency is a basic idea that is significant in a variety of disciplines, such as business, computer science, physics, psychology, and mathematics. It guarantees results that are trustworthy and predictable and contributes to the establishment of predictability and order in the outside environment. It's a characteristic linked to accountability, consistency, and dependability in a person's actions.

A little child named Jack used to dwell in a small village tucked away in the undulating hills of a far-off place. Jack was an aspirational and diligent young man with a strong drive to succeed in life. He worked on his father's farm for most of his days, taking care of the animals and crops while hoping to one day leave the hamlet and become well-known.

Jack once encountered a knowledgeable old guy who was strolling through the hamlet while he was out in the fields. When the elderly guy came to a stop beneath a tree's shade, he asked Jack if he had any extra water to give. Jack complied, and as he sat down to talk with the elderly guy, he couldn't resist telling him about his goals and objectives.

After Jack was finished, the elderly man observed, "My boy, you have a great desire to make something of yourself, and that is a good thing." The man listened carefully. However, if you want to fulfill your dreams, there is one thing you need to learn."

"And what is that?" Jack inquired, curious to find out.

"Consistency," the elderly guy answered. "As you can see, success depends on consistency. The one thing that sets the genuinely exceptional apart from the rest of us is this. No matter how big or small our goals may be, consistency is what enables us to reach them."

Jack paid close attention and realized the elderly man was correct. Jack vowed to himself that day to be consistent in everything he did. Every day, he put forth a lot of effort on the farm, and no matter how hard things became, he never gave up.

Jack's diligence and perseverance became apparent as the years went by. His crops were the talk of the town as he rose to prominence as one of the most prosperous farmers. Everyone who knew him appreciated and respected him, and he was appreciative of the elderly man who had instilled in him the value of constancy.

However, Jack's tale did not finish there. Eventually, driven by his desire to accomplish even more, he left the town and set out into the world. He launched his own company and put in a lot of effort to see it through to success. And once more, his perseverance was rewarded. He created a flourishing company that was well-known across the nation for its high-caliber goods and first-rate customer support.

As the years passed, Jack emerged as one of the most prosperous and well-liked individuals in the nation. And all those years ago, the old man had taught him lessons he would never forget. He was aware that consistency was essential to his success; therefore, no matter how challenging the circumstances were, he never forgot to uphold his moral standards.

Thus, Jack's tale serves as a warning to each and every one of us about the value of consistency. It is the one characteristic that sets the genuinely great apart from the rest of us, and it holds the secret to realizing all of our aspirations, no matter how lofty.

How To Beat Procrastination

As we become more conscious of our time management, we probably discover that we have been prone to procrastination. This has occasionally been really bad for me. While pursuing my bachelor's degree, I headed a band, like many young adults who enjoy music. This was fantastic, especially in light of the University's active music scene and the abundance of options for performing in front of an audience. We played once in the year that we were together. This was solely because I had a terrible habit of putting things off, rarely showing up for practice, and occasionally even leaving early. Nothing much changed for us when we finally broke up. However, it served as a forewarning to me that things were about to spiral out of control.

According to Abbasi and Alghamdi (2015), procrastination takes up more than 25% of most people's working days, costing companies an estimated $10,000 per employee annually. Measuring a common problem is simpler. Several factors that lead to procrastination were identified in the same study. Among the most prominent ones are: ● Experiencing Overwhelm.

● Weak Skills in Organisation.

● Having insufficient positive motivation or feeling demotivated.

● An obsession with perfection.

● A negative view of yourself.

● A fear of not succeeding.

If you can identify with one or more of the points, don't be hard on yourself. These can be the main causes of your procrastination, along with other things. But you can deal with them, no matter how severe they are. This includes the underlying causes of procrastination as well. I'll go over a few choices and tools that can help you get over this obstacle.

Curiously, a final lesson from our earlier source is a few approaches to procrastination management. The main focus of their conclusion is on the benefits of therapy. And this has some worth! The proper perception of therapy is now one of a self-care activity as opposed to a critique of an individual's abilities. Therefore, receiving individual counseling would be beneficial if you currently practice it or if your place of employment has a therapist. Other, less time-consuming choices exist. Abbasi&Alghamdi, for instance, mention that one effective counteragent is to define precise and concise goals, which we did in Chapter 2!

A broader strategy may involve changing the way we handle our jobs at work. A project frequently appears bigger and meaner than it is. Try breaking the project up into manageable chunks and completing them rather than letting that consume you. It's a meager triumph. However, it's something that could spur more advancement. Forcing ourselves to do a tedious chore in exchange for a reward is another wise concept. Even something as small as a snack will work. Using productivity apps is an additional choice that frequently combines this with other techniques like the Eisenhower Matrix or the Pomodoro Method.

We can also combine different ideas from above. We have a better chance of avoiding ineffective behaviors when we use a blended strategy. While attempting to address the core issues through talk therapy, you can implement a reward system. Starting small and depending on an app is an option. Like many wonderful things in life, there are several approaches to time management. Choose one based on your personality and workflow!

Dividing projects into manageable components is another excellent strategy for dealing with procrastination tendencies. Acts, for instance, may be used to organize a novel of 90,000 words. It can also be comprehended chapter by chapter or even divided into paragraphs! When you apply the same idea to your work, it frequently appears less daunting. Handle each of these fractions as if it were its own assignment, and give yourself credit for it. It should be noted that routine-building benefits greatly from this concept as well. Having a few simple, easy-to-finish hobbies might effectively 'stack' with other habits.

So, we've worked out how to deal with ourselves, losing concentration and spending time unproductively. But what happens when external influences come into play? It's reductionist to suppose work can be performed in a vacuum: Noises, guests, and itinerary changes are all too usual in an office atmosphere. So, let's figure out what to do when these actors endanger our productivity!

CHAPTER 9 CONSISTENCY AND HABIT FORMATION

Create and sustain time management techniques that become automatic.

We may feel overworked and unproductive after juggling employment, family, personal aspirations, and leisure. So do not worry! Your ability to manage your time successfully depends on creating and adhering to excellent habits that become second nature. This extensive guide will dig thoroughly into the art of habit development and present you with a road map for developing a life of success, balance, and productivity.

Educating Oneself on the Science of Habits

Let's first comprehend how habits are formed scientifically before going on to the practical steps. The brain automates actions through habits, conserving mental energy. They are made up of three parts: cue, routine, and reward. Building strong time management techniques requires knowing these components.

Clearing Your Goals

Setting precise, realistic goals is the core of efficient time management practices.

Determining your goals provides you direction and drive, whether they are for finishing a project, getting in shape, or simply finding more personal time.

Describing It

Now that you can perceive your objectives, it's time to turn them into doable actions. Complex goals may be made less scary and more feasible by breaking them down into smaller, more manageable steps.

Techniques for Prioritization

Tasks are not all created equal. It's crucial to gain the skill to prioritize your to-do list. We'll look at many strategies to assist you in maintaining your concentration on what's vital.

Consistency is Important

The foundation of habit forming is consistency. We'll speak about how to get over hurdles like procrastination and distractions, and we'll give tips on how to keep up your new habits even when life throws you a curve ball.

Tracking and Accountability

Strong motivators include monitoring your progress and sharing your aims with others. The use of digital technologies and hiring a mentor or coach are just a few of the accountability methods that will be explored.

Create a Support System

Maintaining strong time management techniques may be immensely beneficial by surrounding oneself with positive folks who share your aims. We'll speak about the value of having a robust network of friends and family as well as how to establish one.

Self-Compassion Development

There will always be errors and failures. You can heal from mistakes without letting them block your growth by fostering self-compassion.

Taking Stock of Success

Your dedication to your time management habits will be increased if you appreciate and acknowledge your victories along the path. The momentum required for long-lasting change is built by tiny accomplishments.

It may first appear tough to adopt efficient time management strategies into your daily routine, but with commitment and persistence, they will become automatic. Be patient with yourself since new habits take time to form. You're well on your way to turning your life into one of productivity, balance, and success by sticking to the instructions in this in-depth manual.

So, let's start this revolutionary experience together. Embrace the effect of habits and witness how your life evolves into a masterpiece of time well-spent and successes.

Wrapping up

In this chapter, we've covered the role of leadership in time management and how you may lead by example and develop a productive team. By modeling good time management practices, communicating expectations clearly, providing training and support, recognizing and rewarding accomplishments, and fostering a culture of productivity, Remember that good leadership needs continual effort and attention, so be sure to reflect on your progress periodically and make modifications as needed.

Exercise: Conduct a Time Audit

One strategy to improve your time management abilities as a leader is to do a time audit. This activity will help you evaluate how you presently spend your time and where you may make improvements to optimize your schedule.

Instructions:

1. Take a week-long period (ideally a workweek) and track your time using a time-tracking app or a pen and paper.

2. Categorize your activities into separate buckets, such as meetings, emails, project work, socializing, and administrative responsibilities.

3. Analyze the data and identify places where you can optimize your time. For instance, you may find that you spend a lot of time attending meetings that might be shortened or removed or that you're spending too much time on administrative work that could be transferred to someone else.

4. Develop a plan for how you may change your schedule to optimize your time. This can include distributing chores, minimizing meeting times, or cutting off particular time periods for undisturbed work.

5. Implement your plan and track your success. Monitor your time usage periodically and make modifications as needed to improve your schedule and increase productivity.

By completing a time audit and making adjustments to improve your schedule, you can lead by example and demonstrate appropriate time management techniques to your staff.

www.ingramcontent.com/pod-product-compliance
Lightning Source LLC
Chambersburg PA
CBHW052150110526
44591CB00012B/1926